PASSAGES

THE PAINTINGS OF SUSAN SEDDON BOULET

1999 ENGAGEMENT CALENDAR

Catalog No. 99188
Published by Pomegranate
Box 6099, Rohnert Park, California 94927
© 1998 The Susan Eleanor Boulet Trust

Available in Canada from Firefly Books Ltd.,
3680 Victoria Park Avenue, Willowdale, Ontario M2H 3K1
Available in the U.K. and mainland Europe from Pomegranate Europe Ltd.,
Fullbridge House, Fullbridge, Maldon, Essex CM9 4LE, England
Available in Australia from Boobook Publications Pty. Ltd.,
P.O. Box 163 or Freepost 1, Tea Gardens 2324
Available in New Zealand from Randy Horwood Ltd.,
P.O. Box 32-077, Devonport, Auckland
Available in Asia (including the Middle East), Africa, and Latin America from
Pomegranate International Sales, 113 Babcombe Drive,
Thornhill, Ontario L3T 1M9, Canada

Pomegranate also publishes Susan Seddon Boulet's paintings in notecards, holiday cards, postcards, books of postcards, posters, bookmarks, art magnets, and gift enclosures, as well as in the books *Buffalo Gals, Won't You Come Out Tonight, Susan Seddon Boulet: The Goddess Paintings, Shaman: The Paintings of Susan Seddon Boulet*, and the 1999 calendars *Shaman, Unicorns,* and *Goddesses.* Our full-color catalog showing our wide selection of 1999 calendars is available for one dollar. We offer our other full-color catalogs (illustrating our notecards, boxed notes, notecard folios, postcards, books of postcards, address books, books of days, posters, art magnets, knowledge cards, bookmarks, journals, and books) for nominal fees.
For more information on obtaining catalogs and ordering, please write to
Pomegranate, Box 6099, Rohnert Park, California 94927.
www. pomegranate.com

Cover design by Sandi Talbot
Front cover: *Eagle Woman,* 1988

All astronomical data supplied in this calendar are expressed in Greenwich Mean Time (GMT).

BIBLIOGRAPHY

Bierhorst, John, ed. *In the Trail of the Wind*. New York: Farrar, Straus & Giroux, 1971.

Curtis, Natalie. *The Indian's Book*. New York: Dover Publications, Inc., 1968. (Unabridged, unaltered republication of the second edition, published by Harper and Brothers in 1923. First edition, 1907.)

Day, A. Grove. *The Sky Clears*. Lincoln, Nebraska: University of Nebraska Press, 1951.

Densmore, Frances. *Pawnee Music*. Bureau of American Ethnology, Bulletin 93. Washington, D.C.: Government Printing Office, 1929.

———*Teton Sioux Music*. Bureau of American Ethnology, Bulletin 61. Washington, D.C.: Government Printing Office, 1918.

———*Yunan and Yaqui Music*. Bureau of American Ethnology, Bulletin 110. Washington, D.C.: Government Printing Office, 1932.

Halifax, Joan. *Shamanic Voices*. New York: Arkana, 1971.

Kalweit, Holgar. *Dreamtime and Innerspace*. Translated from German by Werner Wunsche. Boston and London: Shambhala, 1988.

Kroeber, A. L. *Handbook of the Indians of California*. Berkeley: California Book Company, 1925.

Levitas, Gloria, Frank R. Vivelo, and Jacqueline J. Vivelo. *American Indian Prose and Poetry: We Wait in Darkness*. New York: G. P. Putnam's Sons, 1974.

McLuhan, T. C. *Touch the Earth*. New York: Outerbridge & Dienstfrey, 1971.

Neihardt, John G. *Black Elk Speaks*. Lincoln, Nebraska, 1961.

O'Bryan, Aileen. *Navaho Indian Myths*. New York: Dover Publications, Inc., 1993. Originally *The Dîné: Origin Myths of the Navaho Indians*. United States Government Printing Office, Washington, D.C., Bulletin 163 of the Bureau of American Ethnology of the Smithsonian Institute, 1956.

Parker, Arthur C. *Parker on the Iroquois*. Syracuse, New York: Syracuse University Press, 1968. All quotes from "The Code of Handsome Lake, the Seneca Prophesy" originally published as a New York State Museum *Bulletin* around 1911.

Preuss, Konrad Theodor. *Die Religion der Doraindianer*. Volume 1, 1912.

Rothenberg, Jerome, ed. *Shaking the Pumpkin*. Garden City, New York: Doubleday & Company, 1972.

Seattle Art Museum. *The Spirit Within: Northwest Coast Native Art from the John H. Hauberg Collection*. Seattle, Washington: Seattle Art Museum, 1995.

Seler, Eduard. *Gesammelte Abhandlunger*. Volume 2, 1902–1905.

Turner, Frederick W., III. *The Portable North American Indian Reader*. New York: The Viking Press, 1973, 4.

Voth, H. R. *Field Museum of Natural History Anthropological Publications*, 1903.

Boxing Day Observed (Canada)

m o n d a y

28 | 362

Electrical Mess

t u e s d a y

29 | 363

w e d n e s d a y

30 | 364

OPEN Sesame

The day has risen,

Go I to behold the dawn,

Hao! you maidens!

Go behold the dawn!

The white-rising!

The yellow-rising!

It has become light.

—Hopi [Bierhorst, p. 165]

t h u r s d a y

31 | 365

New Year's Day

f r i d a y

| 1

Full Moon

s a t u r d a y

2 | 2

UNTITLED, 1972

S	M	T	W	T	F	S
					1	2
3	4	5	6	7	8	9
10	11	12	13	14	15	16
17	18	19	20	21	22	23
24	25	26	27	28	29	30
31					JANUARY	

s u n d a y

3 | 3

A woman named Be was alone in the bush one day in Namibia, when she saw a herd of giraffes running before an approaching thunderstorm. The rolling beat of their hooves grew louder and mingled in her head with the sound of sudden rain. Suddenly a song she had never heard before came to her, and she began to sing.

Gauwa (the great god) told her it was a medicine song. Be went home and taught the song to her husband, Tike. They sang and danced it together. And it was, indeed, a song for trancing. A medicine song. Tike taught it to others, who passed it on.

—as described by Marguerite Anne Biesele in *Folklore and Ritual of !Kung Hunter-Gatherers* [Cambridge, 1975]

AFRICAN QUEEN, 1973

S	M	T	W	T	F	S
					1	2
3	4	5	6	7	8	9
10	11	12	13	14	15	16
17	18	19	20	21	22	23
24	25	26	27	28	29	30
31					JANUARY	

monday
4 | 4

7:00 Haircut/Color ✓
tuesday
5 | 5

Call about Chiropractic ✓
wednesday
6 | 6

Open Sesame. Spray ✓
thursday
7 | 7

Schedule DMV ✓
friday
8 | 8

Call Terry @ Good Nature
Last Quarter
saturday
9 | 9

1:00 w/ Terry
sunday
10 | 10

m o n d a y

| | 11

Go to DMV

t u e s d a y

| 2 | 12

Go to Mom: Dads

w e d n e s d a y

| 3 | 13

Everything that has life has spirit as well as fleshly form. All things have nagi—*soul. Rocks and animals have the power to appear in the form of man, and to speak to man in dream or in vision. It is from Wakan-Tanka that they have power and wisdom.*

—as told by Huhuseca-ska (White Bone), Zintkala Maza (Iron Bird), and Mato-Nazin (Standing-Bear) of the Dakota [Curtis, p. 61]

t h u r s d a y

| 4 | 14

Martin Luther King Jr.'s Birthday

f r i d a y

| 5 | 15

s a t u r d a y

| 6 | 16

UNTITLED, 1973

S	M	T	W	T	F	S
					1	2
3	4	5	6	7	8	9
10	11	12	13	14	15	16
17	18	19	20	21	22	23
24	25	26	27	28	29	30
31					**JANUARY**	

Mom: Dad to Redding

New Moon

s u n d a y

| 7 | 17

monday

18 | 18

tuesday

19 | 19

Soon feeling the darkness, Yolkai
Estan formed a circle, shaping
it of turquoise and white shells.
Over this she held a rock of
crystal, held it until a fire burst
forth, a blaze that grew so hot,
so bright, that with the help of the
Holy People, White Shell Woman
pushed it further and further away,
higher and higher into the spaces
of heaven. So it happened that
Yolkai Estan, she who had been
born at the time of trouble, she
who had arrived attended by
rainbows, brought light to the Earth.

—Navajo

wednesday

20 | 20

thursday

21 | 21

5:05 DMV

friday

22 | 22

Lupe leaves Early

* 8:00 Chiropractic

saturday

23 | 23

UNTITLED, 1974

S	M	T	W	T	F	S
					1	2
3	4	5	6	7	8	9
10	11	12	13	14	.15	16
17	18	19	20	21	22	23
24	25	26	27	28	29	30
31					JANUARY	

First Quarter

sunday

24 | 24

monday

25 | 25

tuesday

26 | 26

wednesday

27 | 27

*Then there came from the sea
a mighty flood. Many were
drowned, and men became fewer.
And when men had thus become
fewer, two old women debated:
"Better to be without day," said
one, "if thus we may be without
death." "No," said the other,
"let us have both light and death."
And as she spoke, it was so: light
came, and death.*

—from Knud Rasmussen, *Eskimo
Folk-Tales* [London, 1921]

thursday

28 | 28

friday

29 | 29

saturday

30 | 30

UNTITLED, 1974

S	M	T	W	T	F	S
					1	2
3	4	5	6	7	8	9
10	11	12	13	14	15	16
17	18	19	20	21	22	23
24	25	26	27	28	29	30
31					JANUARY	

Full Moon

sunday

31 | 31

monday
1 | 32

tuesday
2 | 33

Then he descended

while the heavens rubbed against
  the earth.

They moved among the four
  lights,

among the four layers of stars.

The world was not lighted;

there was neither day nor night
  nor moon.

Then they perceived that the
  world was being created.

Then creation dawned upon the
  world.

—Translated from the Maya
[Bierhorst, p. 3]

wednesday
3 | 34

thursday
4 | 35

friday
5 | 36

saturday
6 | 37

**ICE KINGDOM
(ARCTIC REALM), 1975**

S	M	T	W	T	F	S
	1	2	3	4	5	6
7	8	9	10	11	12	13
14	15	16	17	18	19	20
21	22	23	24	25	26	27
28						

FEBRUARY

sunday
7 | 38

february

Last Quarter

m o n d a y

8 | 39

t u e s d a y

9 | 40

w e d n e s d a y

10 | 41

The old men

say:

the earth

only endures.

You spoke

truly.

t h u r s d a y

11 | 42

You are right.

Lincoln's Birthday

f r i d a y

12 | 43

—"The Earth Only Endures," sung by
Used-as-a-Shield [Densmore,
Teton Sioux Music, p. 356]

s a t u r d a y

13 | 44

KINGFISHER, 1976

S	M	T	W	T	F	S
	1	2	3	4	5	6
7	8	9	10	11	12	13
14	15	16	17	18	19	20
21	22	23	24	25	26	27
28						

FEBRUARY

Valentine's Day

s u n d a y

14 | 45

february

Presidents' Day

m o n d a y

15 | 46

New Moon

t u e s d a y

16 | 47

Ash Wednesday

w e d n e s d a y

17 | 48

t h u r s d a y

18 | 49

*Woman of the Southern Cross
am I.*

Woman of the first star am I.

Woman of the Star of God am I.

For I go up into the sky.

—Maria Sabina, Mazatec shaman

f r i d a y

19 | 50

s a t u r d a y

20 | 51

APHRODITE, 1976

S	M	T	W	T	F	S
	1	2	3	4	5	6
7	8	9	10	11	12	13
14	15	16	17	18	19	20
21	22	23	24	25	26	27
28						

FEBRUARY

s u n d a y

21 | 52

Washington's Birthday

monday

22 | 53

First Quarter

tuesday

23 | 54

wednesday

24 | 55

Again perhaps
  you expect to sit up high
  in your father's canoe, chief-
woman

and look anew
  around the place
  from where the coppers come

Be careful,
  be careful, chief-woman!

—Haida cradle song,
collected 1912 [Seattle Art
Museum, p. 114]

thursday

25 | 56

friday

26 | 57

saturday

27 | 58

UNTITLED, 1976

S	M	T	W	T	F	S
	1	2	3	4	5	6
7	8	9	10	11	12	13
14	15	16	17	18	19	20
21	22	23	24	25	26	27
28						

FEBRUARY

sunday

28 | 59

monday

1 | 60

Full Moon

tuesday

2 | 61

From Wakan-Tanka, the Great
Mystery, comes all power. It is
from Wakan-Tanka that the Holy
Man has wisdom and the power
to heal and to make holy charms.
Man knows that all healing plants
are given by Wakan-Tanka;
therefore are they holy. So too is
the buffalo holy, because it is the
gift of Wakan-Tanka. The Great
Mystery gave to men all things
for their food, their clothing, and
their welfare. And to man he gave
also the knowledge how to use
these gifts—how to find the holy
healing plants, how to hunt and
surround the buffalo, how to
know wisdom. For all comes
from Wakan-Tanka—all.

—Chief Maza Blaska (Flat-Iron,
meaning a piece of flat iron) of the
Ogallalla Dakota. [Curtis, pp. 38–39]

wednesday

3 | 62

---

thursday

4 | 63

---

friday

5 | 64

UNTITLED, 1977

saturday

6 | 65

S	M	T	W	T	F	S
	1	2	3	4	5	6
7	8	9	10	11	12	13
14	15	16	17	18	19	20
21	22	23	24	25	26	27
28	29	30	31			

MARCH

sunday

7 | 66

m o n d a y

8 | 67

t u e s d a y

9 | 68

Last Quarter

w e d n e s d a y

10 | 69

t h u r s d a y

11 | 70

If you seek to know me, you must look

for me in the clouds. . . .

I am a bird, and I fly high over

the earth. . . .

—Keeshkumun
(Anishinaabe, 1800s)

f r i d a y

12 | 71

s a t u r d a y

13 | 72

UNTITLED 1978

S	M	T	W	T	F	S
	1	2	3	4	5	6
7	8	9	10	11	12	13
14	15	16	17	18	19	20
21	22	23	24	25	26	27
28	29	30	31			

MARCH

s u n d a y

14 | 73

monday

15 | 74

tuesday

16 | 75

St. Patrick's Day
New Moon

wednesday

17 | 76

thursday

18 | 77

*I am now going home, I step upon
another world, I turn and extend
my arms for a friend to lead me,
I pray all may go where I go.
Now the earth is smoky and none
can see the other world [as I do].*

—Iroquois song [Parker, pp. 84–85]

friday

19 | 78

saturday

20 | 79

UNTITLED, 1978

S	M	T	W	T	F	S
	1	2	3	4	5	6
7	8	9	10	11	12	13
14	15	16	17	18	19	20
21	22	23	24	25	26	27
28	29	30	31			

MARCH

Vernal Equinox 1:46 A.M. (GMT)

sunday

21 | 80

monday

22 | 81

tuesday

23 | 82

First Quarter

wednesday

24 | 83

thursday

25 | 84

The outer world
pretends you're not
but the Outside Grandfather
he knows you
oh yes
he's moving toward you.

—from an Asiatic Eskimo song

friday

26 | 85

saturday

27 | 86

THE SEA OF DRAGONS, 1978

S	M	T	W	T	F	S
	1	2	3	4	5	6
7	8	9	10	11	12	13
14	15	16	17	18	19	20
21	22	23	24	25	26	27
28	29	30	31			
					MARCH	

Palm Sunday

sunday

28 | 87

monday
29 | 88

tuesday
30 | 89

In wild flight

I sent the swallows

in wild flight

I made them go

in wild flight

before the clouds were gathered

In wild flight

I sent my horse

in wild flight

a swallow flying running

in wild flight

before the clouds were gathered

　　　　—Sioux Metamorphoses
[Densmore, *Teton Sioux Music*]

Passover (begins at sunset)
Full Moon

wednesday
31 | 90

thursday
1 | 91

Good Friday

friday
2 | 92

saturday
3 | 93

AGE OF THE AVATAR, 1978

S	M	T	W	T	F	S
					1	2	3
4	5	6	7	8	9	10
11	12	13	14	15	16	17
18	19	20	21	22	23	24
25	26	27	28	29	30	

APRIL

Easter Sunday

sunday
4 | 94

Sacred is the act by which my
hands are browned,

It is the act by which I offer my
prayer.

Sacred is the act by which my
hands are blackened,

It is the act by which I offer my
prayer.

Sacred is the act by which my face
is browned,

It is the act by which I offer my
prayer.

Sacred is the act by which my face
is blackened,

It is the act by which I offer my
prayer.

Sacred is the light that falls upon
my face,

The day on which my prayers are
finished.

—Black Bear song of the Osage
[Day, p. 108]

COMPANIONS, 1979

S	M	T	W	T	F	S
				1	2	3
4	5	6	7	8	9	10
11	12	13	14	15	16	17
18	19	20	21	22	23	24
25	26	27	28	29	30	
					APRIL	

Easter Monday (Canada)

monday

5 | 95

tuesday

6 | 96

wednesday

7 | 97

thursday

8 | 98

Last Quarter

friday

9 | 99

saturday

10 | 100

sunday

11 | 101

monday

12 | 102

tuesday

13 | 103

wednesday

14 | 104

thursday

15 | 105

New Moon

friday

16 | 106

saturday

17 | 107

sunday

18 | 108

While I stood there, I saw more than I can tell, and I understood more than I saw; for I was seeing in a sacred manner the shapes of all things in the spirit, and the shape of all shapes as they must live together like one being.

—Ogallalla Sioux holy man
Black Elk [Neihardt]

UNICORN, 1979

S	M	T	W	T	F	S
				1	2	3
4	5	6	7	8	9	10
11	12	13	14	15	16	17
18	19	20	21	22	23	24
25	26	27	28	29	30	

APRIL

monday

19 | 109

tuesday

20 | 110

wednesday

21 | 111

*Everything the Power of the
World does is done in a circle.
The sky is round, and I have
heard that the earth is round like
a ball, and so are all the stars.
The wind, in its greatest power,
whirls. Birds make their nests in
circles, for theirs is the same
religion as ours.*

—Ogallalla Sioux holy man
Black Elk [Neihardt]

Earth Day
First Quarter

thursday

22 | 112

friday

23 | 113

UNTITLED, 1979

saturday

24 | 114

S	M	T	W	T	F	S
				1	2	3
4	5	6	7	8	9	10
11	12	13	14	15	16	17
18	19	20	21	22	23	24
25	26	27	28	29	30	

APRIL

sunday

25 | 115

monday

26 | 116

tuesday

27 | 117

wednesday

28 | 118

thursday

29 | 119

Come, you supernatural ones!
The most famous Kusiut of all
[Thunder] is about to dance!

—Nuxalk song, collected 1922
[Seattle Art Museum, p. 184]

Full Moon

friday

30 | 120

saturday

1 | 121

UNTITLED, 1979

S	M	T	W	T	F	S
						1
2	3	4	5	6	7	8
9	10	11	12	13	14	15
16	17	18	19	20	21	22
23	24	25	26	27	28	29
30	31				**M A Y**	

sunday

2 | 122

monday

3 | 123

tuesday

4 | 124

I dreamt about you last night

you were walking on the pebbles
   of the beach

with me

I dreamt about you

as if I had awakened

I followed you

beautiful

as a young seal

I wanted you like a hunter

lusting after a very young seal

who plunges in, feeling pursued.

That's how it was

for me

—from Knud Rasmussen,
The Netsilik Eskimos, 1931

Cinco de Mayo

wednesday

5 | 125

thursday

6 | 126

friday

7 | 127

Last Quarter

saturday

8 | 128

UNTITLED, 1979

S	M	T	W	T	F	S
						1
2	3	4	5	6	7	8
9	10	11	12	13	14	15
16	17	18	19	20	21	22
23	24	25	26	27	28	29
30	31					MAY

Mother's Day

sunday

9 | 129

monday

10 | 130

tuesday

11 | 131

wednesday

12 | 132

thursday

13 | 133

*For long years I have kept this
   beauty with me*

It has been my life.

It is sacred.

*I give it now that coming
   generations may know the
   truth. . . .*

   —Sandoval's Prayer, Dîne [O'Bryan]

friday

14 | 134

Armed Forces Day
New Moon

saturday

15 | 135

LEO, 1979

S	M	T	W	T	F	S
						1
2	3	4	5	6	7	8
9	10	11	12	13	14	15
16	17	18	19	20	21	22
23	24	25	26	27	28	29
30	31					**M A Y**

sunday

16 | 136

monday

17 | 137

tuesday

18 | 138

wednesday

19 | 139

thursday

20 | 140

Let us see, is this real,

let us see, is this real,

This life I am living?

You, Gods, who dwell everywhere,

Let us see, is this real,

This life I am living?

—Pawnee [Turner, p. 241]

friday

21 | 141

First Quarter

saturday

22 | 142

UNICORN, 1980

S	M	T	W	T	F	S
						1
2	3	4	5	6	7	8
9	10	11	12	13	14	15
16	17	18	19	20	21	22
23	24	25	26	27	28	29
30	31					**M A Y**

sunday

23 | 143

Victoria Day (Canada)

m o n d a y

24 | 144

t u e s d a y

25 | 145

w e d n e s d a y

26 | 146

I stood here, I stood there,

The Clouds are speaking,

I say, "You are the ruling power,

*I do not understand, I only know
what I am told,*

*You are the ruling power, You are
now speaking,*

The power is yours, O heavens."

—from Densmore, *Pawnee Music*

t h u r s d a y

27 | 147

f r i d a y

28 | 148

YOUNG MEN SHALL HAVE
THEIR VISIONS, 1982

s a t u r d a y

29 | 149

S	M	T	W	T	F	S
						1
2	3	4	5	6	7	8
9	10	11	12	13	14	15
16	17	18	19	20	21	22
23	24	25	26	27	28	29
30	31					**M A Y**

Memorial Day
Full Moon

s u n d a y

30 | 150

Memorial Day Observed

m o n d a y

3 1 | 151

t u e s d a y

1 | 152

My words are tied in one
With the great mountains,
With the great rocks,
With the great trees,
In one with my body
And my heart.

Do you all help me
With supernatural power,
And you, day,
And you, night!
All of you see me
One with this world!

—Yokuts song

w e d n e s d a y

2 | 153

t h u r s d a y

3 | 154

f r i d a y

4 | 155

OSIRIS, 1982

S	M	T	W	T	F	S
		1	2	3	4	5
6	7	8	9	10	11	12
13	14	15	16	17	18	19
20	21	22	23	24	25	26
27	28	29	30			

JUNE

s a t u r d a y

5 | 156

s u n d a y

6 | 157

Last Quarter

7 | 158

t u e s d a y

8 | 159

Spirits come to man in dreams
and in waking visions. When the
spirit comes to man in a dream,
it may be thus: a song is heard
on the air, then a form appears.
This form is of a man, often
dressed or painted in some
particular or strange way. It is
a spirit, who gives to the man a
message, a teaching, or a song.
When he turns to go, he takes,
in disappearing, whatsoever form
may be his own,—if he be
animal, he will take the form of
bear, buffalo, or bird—whatever
his nature.

—as told by Huhuseca-ska (White
Bone), Zintkala Maza (Iron Bird),
and Mato-Nazin (Standing Bear),
of the Dakota [Curtis, p. 61]

w e d n e s d a y

9 | 160

t h u r s d a y

10 | 161

f r i d a y

11 | 162

s a t u r d a y

12 | 163

I HEARD THE OWL
CALL MY NAME, 1982

S	M	T	W	T	F	S
			1	2	3	4	5
6	7	8	9	10	11	12
13	14	15	16	17	18	19
20	21	22	23	24	25	26
27	28	29	30			

JUNE

New Moon

s u n d a y

13 | 164

Flag Day

14 | 165

15 | 166

Ah, *flowers that we wear!*

Ah, *songs that we raise!*

—*we are on our way to the*
   Realm of Mystery!

If *only for one day,*

let *us be together, my friends!*

We *must leave our flowers*
   behind us,

We *must leave our songs:*

and *yet the earth remains*
   unchanged.

My *friends, enjoy! Friends!*
   Enjoy!

—Aztec [Bierhorst, p. 101]

16 | 167

17 | 168

18 | 169

UNTITLED, 1983
from *The Candlemaker and*
Other Tales

S	M	T	W	T	F	S
		1	2	3	4	5
6	7	8	9	10	11	12
13	14	15	16	17	18	19
20	21	22	23	24	25	26
27	28	29	30			

J U N E

19 | 170

Father's Day
First Quarter

20 | 171

june

Summer Solstice 7:49 P.M. (GMT)

m o n d a y

21 | 172

t u e s d a y

22 | 173

w e d n e s d a y

23 | 174

In the beginning of all things,
wisdom and knowledge were with
the animals; for Tirawa, the One
Above, did not speak directly
to man. He sent certain animals
to tell men that he showed himself
through the beasts, and that from
them, and from the stars and the
sun and the moon, man should
learn. Tirawa spoke to man
through his works.

—Chief Letakots-Lesa of the
Pawnee tribe [Curtis]

t h u r s d a y

24 | 175

f r i d a y

25 | 176

s a t u r d a y

26 | 177

BROTHER FRANCIS, 1984

S	M	T	W	T	F	S
		1	2	3	4	5
6	7	8	9	10	11	12
13	14	15	16	17	18	19
20	21	22	23	24	25	26
27	28	29	30			

JUNE

s u n d a y

27 | 178

Full Moon

m o n d a y

28 | 179

t u e s d a y

29 | 180

Here they meet

her words and the eagle's

w e d n e s d a y

30 | 181

we hear them together

together they make great sound

Eagle words

fading

Canada Day (Canada)

t h u r s d a y

1 | 182

far above the water of life

Mother words

from deep down

sighing away through the vaults
    of the sky.

f r i d a y

2 | 183

—"The Eagle Above Us"
[Preuss, p. 43]

s a t u r d a y

3 | 184

EAGLE WOMAN, 1986

S	M	T	W	T	F	S
				1	2	3
4	5	6	7	8	9	10
11	12	13	14	15	16	17
18	19	20	21	22	23	24
25	26	27	28	29	30	31
					JULY	

Independence Day

s u n d a y

4 | 185

Susan Seddon Boulet
1987

Independence Day Holiday

m o n d a y

5 | 186

Last Quarter

t u e s d a y

6 | 187

w e d n e s d a y

7 | 188

t h u r s d a y

8 | 189

The raven cried for me

the raven cried for me

the raven's cry came to my mouth

all around the world

  —Kwakwaka'wakw song, collected
   1895 [Seattle Art Museum, p. 212]

f r i d a y

9 | 190

s a t u r d a y

10 | 191

RAVEN, 1987

S	M	T	W	T	F	S
				1	2	3
4	5	6	7	8	9	10
11	12	13	14	15	16	17
18	19	20	21	22	23	24
25	26	27	28	29	30	31
						JULY

s u n d a y

11 | 192

monday

12 | 193

Songs are thoughts, sung out with
the breath when people are moved
by great forces and ordinary
speech no longer suffices. Man is
moved just like an ice floe sailing
here and there out in the current.
His thoughts are driven by a
flowing force when he feels joy,
when he feels fear, when he feels
sorrow. Thought can wash over
him like a flood, making his
breath come in gasps and his
heart throb. Something, like an
abatement in the weather, will
keep him thawed up and then it
will happen that we, who always
think that we are small, will feel
still smaller. And we will fear to
use words. But it will happen that
the words we need will come of
themselves. When the words we
want to use shoot up of themselves—we get a new song.

—Orpingalik, a Netsilingmint
Eskimo [Kalweit, p. 144]

New Moon

tuesday

13 | 194

wednesday

14 | 195

thursday

15 | 196

friday

16 | 197

saturday

17 | 198

MEDICINE DANCE, 1987

S	M	T	W	T	F	S
				1	2	3
4	5	6	7	8	9	10
11	12	13	14	15	16	17
18	19	20	21	22	23	24
25	26	27	28	29	30	31

JULY

sunday

18 | 199

monday

19 | 200

First Quarter

tuesday

20 | 201

wednesday

21 | 202

The jaguar is an important figure
in South American mythology,
shamanism, and folk belief.
The jaguar is a favorite helper
of shamans, used especially in
healing ceremonies. Shamans can
shapeshift into jaguars at need.
In various Brazilian myths, the
jaguar is credited with giving fire
and also the first crafts to
humankind. It is said the jaguar
is a nocturnal animal because the
moon once helped a jaguar escape
as he was fleeing from a hunter.

—Michael Babcock

thursday

22 | 203

friday

23 | 204

saturday

24 | 205

JAGUAR WOMAN, 1987

S	M	T	W	T	F	S
				1	2	3
4	5	6	7	8	9	10
11	12	13	14	15	16	17
18	19	20	21	22	23	24
25	26	27	28	29	30	31
						JULY

sunday

25 | 206

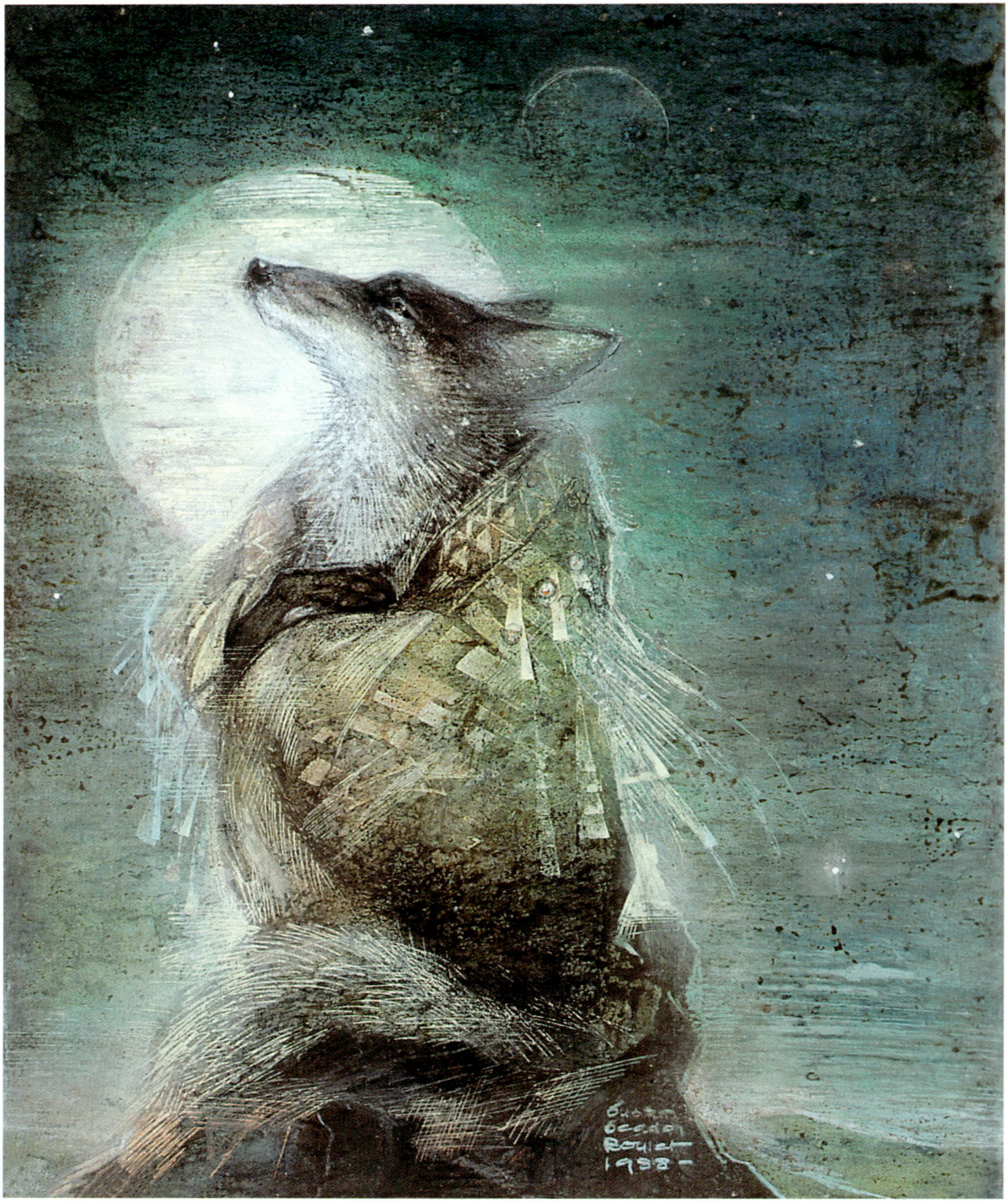

monday

26 | 207

tuesday

27 | 208

Full Moon

wednesday

28 | 209

thursday

29 | 210

The howling coyote took up common dirt and scattered it toward the sky. He caused the dirt to become stars and the rainbow.

—Song in the Yuma Deer Dance [Densmore, *Yuman and Yaqui Music*, p. 145]

friday

30 | 211

saturday

31 | 212

COYOTE WOMAN, 1988

S	M	T	W	T	F	S
1	2	3	4	5	6	7
8	9	10	11	12	13	14
15	16	17	18	19	20	21
22	23	24	25	26	27	28
29	30	31				

AUGUST

sunday

1 | 213

monday

2 | 214

tuesday

3 | 215

Last Quarter

wednesday

4 | 216

thursday

5 | 217

O great expanse of the blue sky,

See me roaming here

Again on the war-path, lonely;

I trust in you, protect me!

—Coyote Warrior-song of
Lukitawika-wari (Rider-Around-the-
Great-Heaven-Domed-Lodge) of the
Chawi band of Pawnee [Curtis, p. 112]

friday

6 | 218

saturday

7 | 219

RIDING THE WIND, 1988

S	M	T	W	T	F	S
1	2	3	4	5	6	7
8	9	10	11	12	13	14
15	16	17	18	19	20	21
22	23	24	25	26	27	28
29	30	31				

AUGUST

sunday

8 | 220

monday

9 | 221

tuesday

10 | 222

New Moon

wednesday

11 | 223

Just as a shaman can turn into
an animal, in Japan and northern
China foxes are believed to be
shape-shifters, able to take on
the form of a human being. Inari,
the goddess of rice and good
fortune, is a vixen goddess,
sometimes seen in the form of
a fox and usually accompanied
by the fox Kitsune, who is her
messenger.

—Michael Babcock

thursday

12 | 224

friday

13 | 225

saturday

14 | 226

FOX WIND, 1988

S	M	T	W	T	F	S
1	2	3	4	5	6	7
8	9	10	11	12	13	14
15	16	17	18	19	20	21
22	23	24	25	26	27	28
29	30	31				

AUGUST

sunday

15 | 227

monday

16 | 228

tuesday

17 | 229

wednesday

18 | 230

In the house of life I wander
on the pollen path,
With a god of cloud I wander
to a holy place.
With a god ahead I wander
and a god behind
In the house of life I wander
on the pollen path.

—Navajo

First Quarter

thursday .

19 | 231

friday

20 | 232

saturday

21 | 233

TIGER LILY, 1988

S	M	T	W	T	F	S
1	2	3	4	5	6	7
8	9	10	11	12	13	14
15	16	17	18	19	20	21
22	23	24	25	26	27	28
29	30	31				

AUGUST

sunday

22 | 234

Susan Seddon Boulet
1988

m o n d a y

23 | 235

t u e s d a y

24 | 236

w e d n e s d a y

25 | 237

Full Moon

t h u r s d a y

26 | 238

Woman who stops the world am I.

Legendary woman who cures am I.

—Maria Sabina, Mazatec shaman

f r i d a y

27 | 239

s a t u r d a y

28 | 240

EAGLE WOMAN, 1988

S	M	T	W	T	F	S
1	2	3	4	5	6	7
8	9	10	11	12	13	14
15	16	17	18	19	20	21
22	23	24	25	26	27	28
29	30	31				

AUGUST

s u n d a y

29 | 241

Susan Seddon Boulet
1989

monday

30 | 242

tuesday

31 | 243

wednesday

1 | 244

I am the owl.

I sit on the spruce tree.

My coat is gray.

I have big eyes.

My head has two points.

The white smoke from my tobacco can be seen

As I sit on the spruce tree.

—"Another Owl's Song"
[O'Bryan, p. 67]

Last Quarter

thursday

2 | 245

friday

3 | 246

DREAMING THE OWL DREAM, 1989

saturday

4 | 247

S	M	T	W	T	F	S
				1	2	3	4
5	6	7	8	9	10	11
12	13	14	15	16	17	18
19	20	21	22	23	24	25
26	27	28	29	30		

SEPTEMBER

sunday

5 | 248

september

Labor Day (U.S. and Canada)

m o n d a y

6 | 249

t u e s d a y

7 | 250

w e d n e s d a y

8 | 251

How shall I begin my songs

in the blue night that is settling?

In the great night my heart will
go out,

Toward me the darkness comes
rattling.

In the great night my heart will
go out.

—Chant of Owl Woman, medicine
woman of the Papago tribe
[Densmore, in Day, p. 87]

New Moon

t h u r s d a y

9 | 252

Rosh Hashanah (begins at sunset)

f r i d a y

10 | 253

s a t u r d a y

11 | 254

DREAMWORLDS, 1990

S	M	T	W	T	F	S
			1	2	3	4
5	6	7	8	9	10	11
12	13	14	15	16	17	18
19	20	21	22	23	24	25
26	27	28	29	30		

SEPTEMBER

s u n d a y

12 | 255

monday

13 | 256

tuesday

14 | 257

wednesday

15 | 258

thursday

16 | 259

Before talking of holy things,
we prepare ourselves by offerings.
. . . one will fill his pipe and hand
it to the other who will light it and
offer it to the sky and earth . . .
they will smoke together . . .
Then will they be ready to talk.

—Mato-Kuwapi (Chased by Bears),
a Santee-Yanktonai Sioux [Densmore,
Teton Sioux Music, pp. 95–96]

First Quarter

friday

17 | 260

saturday

18 | 261

THE HEALER, 1990

S	M	T	W	T	F	S
				1	2	3	4
5	6	7	8	9	10	11
12	13	14	15	16	17	18
19	20	21	22	23	24	25
26	27	28	29	30		
					SEPTEMBER	

Yom Kippur (begins at sunset)

sunday

19 | 262

monday

20 | 263

tuesday

21 | 264

wednesday

22 | 265

Is that the reason
   of his being winter dancer
Is that the reason
   of his being winter dancer
to join in the winter dance
   with his winter dance song
spreading its wings
   over the world

—Kwakw<u>aka</u>'wakw song,
collected 1895 [Seattle, p. 218]

Autumnal Equinox 11:31 A.M. *(GMT)*

thursday

23 | 266

friday

24 | 267

Full Moon

saturday

25 | 268

GWYDION, 1990

S	M	T	W	T	F	S
				1	2	3	4
5	6	7	8	9	10	11
12	13	14	15	16	17	18
19	20	21	22	23	24	25
26	27	28	29	30		

SEPTEMBER

sunday

26 | 269

monday

27 | 270

tuesday

28 | 271

I have noticed in my life that all
men have a liking for some special
animal, tree, plant, or spot of
earth. If men would pay more
attention to those preferences
and seek what is best to do in
order to make themselves worthy
of that toward which they are so
attracted, they might have dreams
which would purify their lives.
Let a man decide upon his
favorite animal and make a study
of it, learning its innocent ways.
Let him learn to understand its
sounds and motions. The animals
want to communicate with man,
but Wakan-Tanka does not
intend they shall do so directly—
man must do the greater part in
securing an understanding.

—Brave Buffalo [Densmore, *Teton
Sioux Music*, p. 172]

wednesday

29 | 272

thursday

30 | 273

friday

1 | 274

Last Quarter

saturday

2 | 275

**WOLF IS COYOTE'S
BROTHER, 1991**

S	M	T	W	T	F	S
					1	2
3	4	5	6	7	8	9
10	11	12	13	14	15	16
17	18	19	20	21	22	23
24	25	26	27	28	29	30
31					OCTOBER	

sunday

3 | 276

monday

4 | 277

tuesday

5 | 278

A wolf

I considered myself

but

I have eaten nothing

therefore

wednesday

from standing

6 | 279

I am tired out.

A wolf

I considered myself

thursday

but

7 | 280

the owls

are hooting

and

the night I fear.

friday

8 | 281

—"A Wolf I Considered Myself,"
as sung by Gray Hawk [Densmore, p. 339]

New Moon

saturday

IN THE COMPANY
OF WOLVES, 1993

9 | 282

S	M	T	W	T	F	S
					1	2
3	4	5	6	7	8	9
10	11	12	13	14	15	16
17	18	19	20	21	22	23
24	25	26	27	28	29	30
31					OCTOBER	

sunday

10 | 283

Columbus Day Observed
Thanksgiving Day (Canada)

m o n d a y

1 1 | 284

Columbus Day

t u e s d a y

1 2 | 285

w e d n e s d a y

1 3 | 286

Grandfather,

a voice I am going to send.

Hear me.

All over the Universe,

a voice I am going to send.

Hear me,

Grandfather.

I will live.

I have said it.

—Opening Prayer of the Sun Dance
[Densmore, *Teton Sioux Music*, p. 131]

t h u r s d a y

1 4 | 287

f r i d a y

1 5 | 288

FEATHERED SERPENT, 1993
(detail)

S	M	T	W	T	F	S
					1	2
3	4	5	6	7	8	9
10	11	12	13	14	15	16
17	18	19	20	21	22	23
24	25	26	27	28	29	30
31					OCTOBER	

s a t u r d a y

1 6 | 289

First Quarter

s u n d a y

1 7 | 290

All is beautiful where I dream.

All is beautiful where I dream.

I dream amid the Dawn and all is
    beautiful.

I dream amid the White Corn and
    all is beautiful.

I dream amid the Beautiful Goods
    and all is beautiful.

I dream amid the Mixed Waters
    and all is beautiful.

I dream amid the Pollens and all
    is beautiful.

I am the Most-High-Power-
    Whose-Ways-Are-Beautiful.

And I dream that all is beautiful.

    —"The Chant Sung When Hasjelti
    Had a Bad Dream," Dîne [O'Bryan]

ROUSSEAU'S DREAM, 1993

S	M	T	W	T	F	S
					1	2
3	4	5	6	7	8	9
10	11	12	13	14	15	16
17	18	19	20	21	22	23
24	25	26	27	28	29	30
31					OCTOBER	

United Nations Day
Full Moon

In the house with the tortoise
   chair

she will give birth to the pearl

in the beautiful feather

In the house of the goddess who
   sits on a tortoise

she will give birth to the necklace
   of pearls

to the beautiful feathers we are

There she sits on the tortoise

   swelling to give us birth

On your way on your way

child be on your way to me here

you whom I made new

Come here child

come be pearl

be beautiful feather

—Aztec poem to ease birth
[Seler, p. 1045]

THE BIRTH OF RAVEN, 1993

S	M	T	W	T	F	S
					1	2
3	4	5	6	7	8	9
10	11	12	13	14	15	16
17	18	19	20	21	22	23
24	25	26	27	28	29	30
31					OCTOBER	

m o n d a y
25 | 298

t u e s d a y
26 | 299

w e d n e s d a y
27 | 300

t h u r s d a y
28 | 301

f r i d a y
29 | 302

s a t u r d a y
30 | 303

Halloween
Last Quarter

s u n d a y
31 | 304

Sean
golden
Boulet
1993

monday

1 | 305

Election Day

tuesday

2 | 306

I am a life-bringer.

I come to heal

with the ways

of the Wolves.

With the crystal

I will heal,

ha wo ho.

wednesday

3 | 307

I have come

with living waters,

these healing ways

of the Wolves,

the living waters,

the spirit crystal,

ha wo ho.

thursday

4 | 308

—Lebi'd, a Kwakiutl shaman, on his
return from the Land of the Dead
[Kalweit, pp. 223–224]

friday

5 | 309

saturday

6 | 310

LONE WOLF, 1993

S	M	T	W	T	F	S
	1	2	3	4	5	6
7	8	9	10	11	12	13
14	15	16	17	18	19	20
21	22	23	24	25	26	27
28	29	30				

NOVEMBER

sunday

7 | 311

New Moon

m o n d a y

8 | 312

t u e s d a y

9 | 313

*The world before me is restored
in beauty.*

*The world behind me is restored
in beauty.*

*The world below me is restored
in beauty.*

*The world above me is restored
in beauty.*

w e d n e s d a y

10 | 314

*All things around me are restored
in beauty.*

Veterans Day
Remembrance Day (Canada)

t h u r s d a y

11 | 315

My voice is restored in beauty.

It is finished in beauty.

It is finished in beauty.

It is finished in beauty.

f r i d a y

12 | 316

—from Washington Matthews, *The
Mountain Chant: A Navajo Ceremony,*
Fifth Annual Report of the Bureau of
American Ethnology, 1883–1884

s a t u r d a y

13 | 317

TRIPLE GODDESS, 1993

S	M	T	W	T	F	S
	1	2	3	4	5	6
7	8	9	10	11	12	13
14	15	16	17	18	19	20
21	22	23	24	25	26	27
28	29	30				

NOVEMBER

s u n d a y

14 | 318

m o n d a y

15 | 319

First Quarter

t u e s d a y

16 | 320

To the Holy Man comes in youth
the knowledge that he will be
holy. The Great Mystery makes
him to know this. Sometimes it
is the Spirits who tell him. The
Spirits come not in sleep always,
but also when man is awake.
When a Spirit comes it would
seem as though a man stood there,
but when this man has spoken and
goes forth again, none may see
whither he goes. Thus the Spirits.
With the Spirits the Holy Man
may commune always, and they
teach him holy things.

—Chief Maza Blaska (Flat-Iron,
meaning "a flat piece of iron") of the
Ogallala Dakota [Curtis, p. 39]

w e d n e s d a y

17 | 321

t h u r s d a y

18 | 322

f r i d a y

19 | 323

s a t u r d a y

20 | 324

THE NAVIGATOR, 1993

S	M	T	W	T	F	S
	1	2	3	4	5	6
7	8	9	10	11	12	13
14	15	16	17	18	19	20
21	22	23	24	25	26	27
28	29	30				
				NOVEMBER		

s u n d a y

21 | 325

monday
22 | 326

Full Moon

tuesday
23 | 327

wednesday
24 | 328

What I am trying to say is hard to tell and hard to understand . . . unless, unless . . . you have been yourself at the edge of the Deep Canyon and have come back unharmed. Maybe it all depends on something within yourself— whether you are trying to see the Watersnake or the sacred Cornflower, whether you go out to meet death or to Seek Life.

—Elder of the San Juan Pueblo

Thanksgiving Day

thursday
25 | 329

friday
26 | 330

OUT OF CHACO CANYON, 1993
(detail)

saturday
27 | 331

S	M	T	W	T	F	S
	1	2	3	4	5	6
7	8	9	10	11	12	13
14	15	16	17	18	19	20
21	22	23	24	25	26	27
28	29	30				

NOVEMBER

sunday
28 | 332

Last Quarter

monday
29 | 333

tuesday
30 | 334

wednesday
1 | 335

thursday
2 | 336

*Upon a little cloud I ascend;
thus I journey upward. To a holy
place. I go, changing as I pass
through the air.*

—Apache Medicine-song
[Curtis, p. 551]

Hanukkah (begins at sunset)

friday
3 | 337

SLEEP AT CHIPMUNK'S, 1994
from *Buffalo Gals, Won't You
Come Out Tonight*

saturday
4 | 338

S	M	T	W	T	F	S
				1	2	3	4
5	6	7	8	9	10	11
12	13	14	15	16	17	18
19	20	21	22	23	24	25
26	27	28	29	30	31	

DECEMBER

sunday
5 | 339

monday

6 | 340

New Moon

tuesday

7 | 341

wednesday

8 | 342

thursday

9 | 343

I have searched in the darkness, being silent in the great lonely stillness of the dark. So I became an angakop, through visions and dreams and encounters with flying spirits.

—Najagneg, an Eskimo shaman
[Halifax, p. 6]

friday

10 | 344

PYGMY OWLS, 1994
from *Buffalo Gals, Won't You Come Out Tonight*

saturday

11 | 345

S	M	T	W	T	F	S
				1	2	3	4
5	6	7	8	9	10	11
12	13	14	15	16	17	18
19	20	21	22	23	24	25
26	27	28	29	30	31	

DECEMBER

sunday

12 | 346

december

m o n d a y

13 | 347

t u e s d a y

14 | 348

Look at me, friend!

I come to ask for your dress,

for it is your way

that there is nothing for which

you cannot be used,

First Quarter

for you are really willing

to give us your dress.

I come to beg you for this,

Long Life Maker,

I am going to make a basket

out of you.

—Kwakwaka'wakw prayer to the
cedar tree, collected 1895 [Seattle, p. 286]

w e d n e s d a y

15 | 349

t h u r s d a y

16 | 350

f r i d a y

17 | 351

s a t u r d a y

18 | 352

FOREST SPIRIT, 1994

S	M	T	W	T	F	S
				1	2	3	4
5	6	7	8	9	10	11
12	13	14	15	16	17	18
19	20	21	22	23	24	25
26	27	28	29	30	31	

DECEMBER

s u n d a y

19 | 353

december

m o n d a y

20 | 354

t u e s d a y

21 | 355

Winter Solstice 7:44 A.M. (GMT)
Full Moon

w e d n e s d a y

22 | 356

Pleasant it looked,

this newly created world.

Along the entire length and
 breadth

of the earth, our grandmother,

extended the green reflection

of her covering

and the escaping odors

were pleasant to inhale.

—Winnebago, [Turner, p. 238]

t h u r s d a y

23 | 357

Christmas Day Holiday

f r i d a y

24 | 358

Christmas Day

s a t u r d a y

25 | 359

MEDICINE WOMAN, 1994

S	M	T	W	T	F	S
				1	2	3	4
5	6	7	8	9	10	11
12	13	14	15	16	17	18
19	20	21	22	23	24	25
26	27	28	29	30	31	

DECEMBER

Kwanzaa begins
Boxing Day (Canada)

s u n d a y

26 | 360

Susan
Seddon
Boulet
1994

Tasunke-hinto (Blue Horse) is
now very old, but he still sings
the Song of the Wolf. Before he
sings he turns to the west, and,
holding up his hands, calls aloud:
"O West Wind, and ye, my old
comrades, if any be there, listen,
listen to my song!" For he says:
"The East is the white man's
country, but the West is where
we belong, I and the wolves, and
my old friends now long dead.
Perhaps I shall soon be with them."

—Tasunke-hinto of the Dakota
[Curtis, p. 54]

WOLF WIND, 1994

S	M	T	W	T	F	S
						1
2	3	4	5	6	7	8
9	10	11	12	13	14	15
16	17	18	19	20	21	22
23	24	25	26	27	28	29
30	31				JANUARY	

Boxing Day Observed (Canada)

m o n d a y

27 | 361

t u e s d a y

28 | 362

Last Quarter

w e d n e s d a y

29 | 363

t h u r s d a y

30 | 364

f r i d a y

31 | 365

New Year's Day 2000

s a t u r d a y

1 | 1

s u n d a y

2 | 2

1999

JANUARY

S	M	T	W	T	F	S
					1	2
3	4	5	6	7	8	9
10	11	12	13	14	15	16
17	18	19	20	21	22	23
24	25	26	27	28	29	30
31						

MAY

S	M	T	W	T	F	S
						1
2	3	4	5	6	7	8
9	10	11	12	13	14	15
16	17	18	19	20	21	22
23	24	25	26	27	28	29
30	31					

SEPTEMBER

S	M	T	W	T	F	S
			1	2	3	4
5	6	7	8	9	10	11
12	13	14	15	16	17	18
19	20	21	22	23	24	25
26	27	28	29	30		

FEBRUARY

S	M	T	W	T	F	S
	1	2	3	4	5	6
7	8	9	10	11	12	13
14	15	16	17	18	19	20
21	22	23	24	25	26	27
28						

JUNE

S	M	T	W	T	F	S
		1	2	3	4	5
6	7	8	9	10	11	12
13	14	15	16	17	18	19
20	21	22	23	24	25	26
27	28	29	30			

OCTOBER

S	M	T	W	T	F	S
					1	2
3	4	5	6	7	8	9
10	11	12	13	14	15	16
17	18	19	20	21	22	23
24	25	26	27	28	29	30
31						

MARCH

S	M	T	W	T	F	S
	1	2	3	4	5	6
7	8	9	10	11	12	13
14	15	16	17	18	19	20
21	22	23	24	25	26	27
28	29	30	31			

JULY

S	M	T	W	T	F	S
				1	2	3
4	5	6	7	8	9	10
11	12	13	14	15	16	17
18	19	20	21	22	23	24
25	26	27	28	29	30	31

NOVEMBER

S	M	T	W	T	F	S
	1	2	3	4	5	6
7	8	9	10	11	12	13
14	15	16	17	18	19	20
21	22	23	24	25	26	27
28	29	30				

APRIL

S	M	T	W	T	F	S
				1	2	3
4	5	6	7	8	9	10
11	12	13	14	15	16	17
18	19	20	21	22	23	24
25	26	27	28	29	30	

AUGUST

S	M	T	W	T	F	S
1	2	3	4	5	6	7
8	9	10	11	12	13	14
15	16	17	18	19	20	21
22	23	24	25	26	27	28
29	30	31				

DECEMBER

S	M	T	W	T	F	S
			1	2	3	4
5	6	7	8	9	10	11
12	13	14	15	16	17	18
19	20	21	22	23	24	25
26	27	28	29	30	31	

JANUARY

S	M	T	W	T	F	S
						1
2	3	4	5	6	7	8
9	10	11	12	13	14	15
16	17	18	19	20	21	22
23	24	25	26	27	28	29
30	31					

MAY

S	M	T	W	T	F	S
	1	2	3	4	5	6
7	8	9	10	11	12	13
14	15	16	17	18	19	20
21	22	23	24	25	26	27
28	29	30	31			

SEPTEMBER

S	M	T	W	T	F	S
					1	2
3	4	5	6	7	8	9
10	11	12	13	14	15	16
17	18	19	20	21	22	23
24	25	26	27	28	29	30

FEBRUARY

S	M	T	W	T	F	S
		1	2	3	4	5
6	7	8	9	10	11	12
13	14	15	16	17	18	19
20	21	22	23	24	25	26
27	28	29				

JUNE

S	M	T	W	T	F	S
				1	2	3
4	5	6	7	8	9	10
11	12	13	14	15	16	17
18	19	20	21	22	23	24
25	26	27	28	29	30	

OCTOBER

S	M	T	W	T	F	S
1	2	3	4	5	6	7
8	9	10	11	12	13	14
15	16	17	18	19	20	21
22	23	24	25	26	27	28
29	30	31				

MARCH

S	M	T	W	T	F	S
			1	2	3	4
5	6	7	8	9	10	11
12	13	14	15	16	17	18
19	20	21	22	23	24	25
26	27	28	29	30	31	

JULY

S	M	T	W	T	F	S
						1
2	3	4	5	6	7	8
9	10	11	12	13	14	15
16	17	18	19	20	21	22
23	24	25	26	27	28	29
30	31					

NOVEMBER

S	M	T	W	T	F	S
			1	2	3	4
5	6	7	8	9	10	11
12	13	14	15	16	17	18
19	20	21	22	23	24	25
26	27	28	29	30		

APRIL

S	M	T	W	T	F	S
						1
2	3	4	5	6	7	8
9	10	11	12	13	14	15
16	17	18	19	20	21	22
23	24	25	26	27	28	29
30						

AUGUST

S	M	T	W	T	F	S
		1	2	3	4	5
6	7	8	9	10	11	12
13	14	15	16	17	18	19
20	21	22	23	24	25	26
27	28	29	30	31		

DECEMBER

S	M	T	W	T	F	S
					1	2
3	4	5	6	7	8	9
10	11	12	13	14	15	16
17	18	19	20	21	22	23
24	25	26	27	28	29	30
31						

notes